The Dedalus Press

Extracts from the Lost Log-book of Christopher Columbus

Gerry Murphy

EXTRACTS FROM THE LOST LOG-BOOK OF CHRISTOPHER COLUMBUS

GERRY MURPHY

DEDALUS

1999

The Dedalus Press
24 The Heath
Cypress Downs
Dublin 6W
Ireland

© Gerry Murphy and The Dedalus Press, 1999

ISBN 1 901233 30 8 (paper)
ISBN 1 901233 31 6 (bound)

Acknowledgements:
Thanks are due to Val Bogan, Willy Kelly, Valerie Spencer, and all
at MicroMail yet again. Some of these poems have appeared in
Tracks 11, The Cafe Review, Compost, Leabhair Sheáin Uí Thuama,
and *Poetry Now* (Dun Laoghaire)

Dedalus Press books are represented and distributed in the
U.S.A. and Canada by **Dufour Editions Ltd.**, P.O. Box 7,
Chester Springs, Pennsylvania 19425
and in the UK by **Central Books**, 99 Wallis Road, London
E9 5LN

The Dedalus Press receives financial assistance from
An Chomhairle Ealaíon, The Arts Council, Ireland.

Printed in Dublin by Colour Books Ltd

CONTENTS

Fortune

(after Luis De Góngora)

Fortune presents gifts
according to her whims,
not according to the book.
She blinds the prophet in one eye
and gives the village idiot second sight.
When you expect whistles, it's flutes,
when flutes, whistles.

Her circuitous routes cannot be traced
as she distributes honours and millstones.
To the altar boy
she grants riches without precedent
while plunging the archbishop headlong
into penury.
When you expect whistles, it's flutes,
when flutes, whistles.

Because a pauper has stolen an egg
he swings from the gallows
while the Governor short-changes
the hangman once again.
When you expect whistles, it's flutes,
when flutes, whistles.

7

for Maura O'Keeffe

End Of Part One

Dead to the earth dead to the faint wriggle
of Spring through the slagheaps until somehow
a new muse sparks in the familiar gloom
like a faulty cigarette lighter I switch on
the sweet flicker of desire again wind up
the slack coil of lust to singing tightness
begin dreaming of your wet 7% yellow
stock market crashes on derelict lighthouse
news and here's

John Fitzgerald Kennedy almost within arm's
length definitely within range standing up
in an open-top cadillac waving furiously
at me and shouting SHOOT YOU FOOL
SHOOT it's June '63 on Military Hill
I'm ten years of age unarmed except
for a congealed wad of liquorice in my
pocket and anyway my mother is right
beside me squeezing my trigger finger
much too tightly in her excitement.

Onwards and upwards you declared nudging
me towards the pit and the long drop
into unutterable stillness - when I crawled
out it was to John Coltrane faint but soothing
in the distance the agitated shuffling of my
own feet and the weary dole operative still
patiently explaining the revised butter
allowance : "listen earthling. . ."

Intimations Of Mortality

Not long after
the Tooth Fairy stopped
leaving me shiny new pennies
under my pillow,
the Angel of Death,
gathering my mother
into his huge beating wings,
shook a dusty black feather
onto my bed.

Breakthrough

Mexico, 1970.
World Cup, quarter final.
England, two up against West Germany
and cruising.
My brother, quietly gloating,
my father and I plunged
into glum, staring silence.
I go out into the kitchen
to make tea,
West Germany claw one back.
"Too little, too late"
my brother declares.
I go back into the kitchen,
West Germany equalize.
My father and I are led out,
blinking, into the daylight.

In extra-time,
Müller, Der Bomber, scores the winner.
I had never hugged my father,
I haven't hugged him since.

Noli Me Tangere

Just a glance will do
a kiss would be much too much
the weight of your lips.

So It Goes

You know how it happens:
The woman you have been
so eager to meet for so long
is standing in front of you
listening, quite intently, to your
somewhat excited babble
when the tiniest fleck of spittle
exits the side of your mouth,
describes a lovely slow parabola
through the astonished air
and lands plumb on her cheek.
To her eternal credit
she doesn't flinch, even in the slightest
and waits until you are out of sight
before reaching for her handkerchief.

Fuckfuckfuckfuckfuckfuckfuckfuckfuckfuck.

The Ferbane Haiku

Long live nothingness
beyond this puny heart-song
this wretched wheezing.

Bite your whining tongue
the loveliest woman here
is looking at you.

Cancel the doctor
this naked conversation
is healing enough.

Down With Telephones

(i) Pacing

Pacing this room,
as if pacing
its exact equivalent
in area in Antarctica,
I recall
the warm bear-like hug
you left me with
the other night,
pause, smile,
pace on.

(ii) Simple Arithmetic

Add to the general air of despondency,
a keen nerve-tingling wind
streaming out from the coast.
Two weeks without
the sound of your voice
or the sweet tilt of your head listening,
two weeks more.

(iii) Love Is..

Even
if I were reduced
to a bleeding eyeball
swivelling on a pointed stick
I would love you,
darling.

(iv) You Can

You can always rely on me
should anything minor crop up:
a dislocation of the pelvis,
political asylum for your aunt,
a weariness with kisses.

(v) Down With Telephones

A warm embrace,
with both arms, just then,
would have said
more than I can ever tell.
Before this night is through,
I may just dig up and hang
Alexander Graham Bell.

Up Yours Gay Byrne

Look on the bright side you can always
blow your brains out during the next
whiter than white detergent commercial
you can turn it down or even turn it
off and storm out into the hallway and
stamp on the landmine you were saving
for the T.V. licence inspector look
on the bright side you could be the third
literary critic this week being beaten prior
to being necklaced you could be lying on
any street in any major town with three
bullet wounds in the head after swearing
under your breath in Danish at a
Conradh na Gaeilge roadblock look
on the bright side any day now during
the next ten million years the sun
is due to expand to seventy times its
present size before dwindling to the
dimensions of an orange we may
have already returned to the Crab Nebula
by then in the form of a superintelligent
vapour it's Urbi et Orbi next after this
word from our sponsors.

Bathroom Vignette

The hot tap
is speaking out of the corner
of its mouth:
"Twenty years steaming service
and for what? for what?"

The cold tap
remains silent, disdainful.

The plughole is all ear.

Labyrinth

(for Thomas McCarthy)

I'm relying on reflections here:
the reception area,
a little like Plato's cave,
each successive glass-panelled door
carrying an image of the sunlit garden,
reversed, corrected, then reversed again;
shifted right, left, right and finally left
onto the steeply angled window-panes
and into the bewildered lens
of the surveillance camera
above the bevelled security mirror.
When you came in, just then,
with your silly questions
and your supercilious grin,
I was rendered speechless
by the grotesque solidity of your presence.

A Mantra for Niamh Connolly

The heron's stillness
against the stark raving weir's
incessant babbling.

Off Summerhill South

(i) Midsummer Vignette

An afternoon breeze
is lifting the curtains
along Douglas Street.
Its huge elemental breathing
fills the room,
cooling our drowsy afterplay.
We lie where we fell,
tangled in half-discarded underwear;
levelled by ecstasy.

(ii) Balaclava

I am perched
on the edge of the bed,
naked except for a pair
of black lace panties
drawn down over my face
in order to inhale
your still warm, still moist smell
again
and again
and again.

(iii) Reductionist Love Poem

Never again
your lovely face in mine
as I wake and blah, blah, blah.
Never again
my arms around you
as I sleep, etcetera, etcetera.
Never again
the rising heat, the cooling passion
and so on.
Never again
those long involved conversations
after midnight
but then, never before.

After Goethe

All nine of them —
the Muses of course —
used to visit me.
I ignored them
for the warmth of your arms,
the sweetness of your kisses.
Then you left me
and they vanished.
I looked about
for a knife or a rope,
anything lethal and to hand
but I was saved by boredom.
Boredom, mother of the Muses.

Ode 38

(after Horace)

Girl, do I detest
that over-elaborate Persian style !
You can keep your fancy garlands
laced up with lime-bark.
And don't break your neck,
racing off to fetch me back
the last rose of summer either.

No more of your delicate attempts
to improve on simple myrtle.
Myrtle suits us nicely,
you pouring, me drinking
under the vine-clad awning.

Daughter of Sarmatia

Here's to your mother's people :
that young Sarmatian princess
buried at Kobiakov on the Don
with her treasury of cult jewellery,
her gleaming battle-axe,
the glittering harness of her horse-team
and across her feet
a flawless youth
strangled at her funeral. .

From the Ancient Greek

(after S.Q.Groden)

The moon is down,
the Pleiades beyond ken.
In the still centre of the night
time is unravelling
and I lie alone, again.

Under The Dog Star

(for M.M)

Imminent synchronicity wakes me.
I open my eyes as the digital clock
displays 3.33.33 a.m.
Beyond the window
a gleaming curve holds up
the dark weight of the moon.
Further out fierce starlight
glitters through from 1347.
Even the dogs are silent —
shot, knifed and bludgeoned into silence.
Thinking of you,
I begin to imagine you
slipping out of the satin hush
of your underwear
into the admiring din of my arms.
Trouble is you are probably awake also,
busy in the sealed off archives of memory
shredding this fiction.

(ii)

Finally I admit to myself
that you will not call
and apart from burning offerings
next to the silent phone,
apart from racking the postman
until he snaps and coughs up
all those letters you insist you sent,
I can do nothing.
So, I sit in the gloom
unravelling steadily,
the gleam of a demented smile
growing brighter and brighter
as I disassemble the rose —
shelovedmeshelovedmenotshelovedmeshe —
reassemble the machine-pistol.

(iii)

This is where
I peel your name
from that battered, much travelled suitcase —
the heart,

where I dissolve whole reels of memories
which played and played
in that obsessive, all hours cinema —
the head.
This is where
I switch off the individually lit photographs
and burn down the dreary warehouse of regret,
where I walk out
into the sweet empty air;
into the desert of myself

Last Night
(after Müller)

As I passed
I wrote "Who, but me?"
reversed in the frost on your window
under the effervescent stars.

In The Beginning

God falls apart,
awareness glitters in the burnished deserts of obsidian,
an astonished sky contemplates an astonished ocean.

Extracts from The Lost Log-Book
of Christopher Columbus

(for John Montague)

Friday August 3rd 1492:

We set out from the bar of Saltes
and travelled with a strong breeze sixty
miles, that is to say fifteen leagues, southward,
before sunset. Afterwards we changed course
to south-west by south, making for the Canaries.

Monday August 6th 1492:

The rudder of the Pinta, whose Captain
is Martín Alonso Pinzón, jumped out of
position. This is said to be the doing
of Gomez Rascón and Cristóbal Quintero,
the owner of the Pinta, who dislike the voyage.

Thursday September 7th 1493:

We set out this morning to continue
our voyage after nearly a month spent
in the Canaries repairing the Pinta.

Friday September 8th:

    All day becalmed.

Sunday September 9th:

    We made fifteen leagues today
but I decided to score up a smaller amount
so as not to alarm the crew who might
take fright at a long voyage.

Monday September 10th:

    Sixty leagues this day and night.
Scored up forty eight.

Friday September 14th:

    The crew of the Niña say they have
seen a tern and a tropic bird neither
of which go more than twenty five leagues
from land.

Saturday September 15th:

Early this evening we saw
a marvellous streak of fire fall into
the sea about four leagues from the ships.

Sun. Sept. 16th:

The weather is like April
in Andalusia.

Thurs. 20th

Two boobies flew to the Santa María
and we saw much weed, a sure sign
of land.

Sun. 23rd:

All day becalmed. The crew grumbled,
saying there would be no wind to carry
them back to Spain.

Tue. 25th:

At sunset Martín Alonso went up
into the poop of the Pinta and called out
most joyfully that he could see land.
I fell on my knees and gave thanks
to God.

Wed. 26th:

What we had taken for land
was a cloud bank.

Thursday 27th:

We saw a tropic bird.

Sat. 29th:

Two boobies.

Tuesday October 2nd:

    A gull.

Wed. 3rd:

    Petrels.

Thur. 4th:

    A frigate bird came to the ship.

Friday 5th:

    Many flying fish.

Tuesday 9th:

    All night we heard birds passing.

Friday 12th:

We sighted land some two leagues away, some naked people appeared.

Saturday 13th:

A petrel and a frigate.

Sunday 14th:

A booby and a tern.

Wednesday 24th

More weed.

Oedipus in Harlem

Yo! Muthafucker

The Fall Of Camelot

By a grassy knoll in Dallas
I lay down and fired.

The Birth of Tyranny
(after Saadi of Shiraz)

On a whim
the Sultan demands a tribute
of half an egg.
His troops roast
one hundred thousand chickens.

Among Thieves

(for Michael O'Riordan)

"There are pickpockets
in the Cathedral"
warned the bishop.
"They may get
to your purses
before we do"
muttered the worried priest.

A Lull in the Eviction Proceedings

(after a photograph by J.M. Synge)

The roof has been ripped off
and two solid swings
from the battering ram
have knocked a cave sized hole
in the gable wall
of the offending dwelling.
The family, a widow and three children,
are being comforted by neighbours,
the odd sly remark notwithstanding.
Someone has made tea
and the Royal Irish Constabulary
with true island hospitality
arc each being offered a cup
The weather has held up well
after all.

The Light In The Window

(after Gene Kerrigan)

Hands busy in a frantic semaphore,
head nodding furiously,
President Robinson found herself
veering towards a catastrophic lull.
She showed President Clinton
·the emigrant's light she keeps
ever-buring in a window.
He stared at the light
for a long time,
trying desperately to think
of something to say.
"It's a low-watt bulb" she assured him.
"Ah" he replied, approvingly, she thought.

The Fort of Rathangan

(after Kuno Meyer)

That rook-loud fort,
hard against the oak-wood,
once it was Bruidge's, then Cathal's,
it was Aed's, then Ailill's,
it was Conaing's, it was Cuilíne's,
it was Maeldúin's.
The fort endures after each in his turn
was tumbled from his perch by Death;
he sorts them, bone from bone
in the ground.

Exit

(after the Irish, ninth century)

With an eye on Heaven
the blind girl
has thrown herself
into the well.

There Is A God

(after Rimbaud)

There is a God
who beams at the damask altarcloths,
who basks in the golden glow of the chalices,
who dozes to the lullaby of Hosannas.
When grieving mothers
come to the church for solace
and let their pennies
rattle into the big iron box,
He wakes up disgruntled
and fires down a dose of clap
at the priest.

A Reading from The Book of Job

(for Val McLoughlin)

(i)

There was a man in the land of Hus
whose name was Job
and that man was simple and upright
and fearing God and avoiding evil.

(ii)

Now upon a certain day
did Job lose his oxen,
his sheep, his asses, his camels,
his servants and his children.
And Job rose up
and rent his garments
and having shaven his head,
fell down upon the ground
and worshipped saying:
"Naked came I out of my mother's womb
and naked shall I return thither.
The Lord gave and the Lord hath taken away.
As it hath pleased the Lord so is it done.
Blessed be the name of the Lord."

(iii)

And the Lord said to Satan:
"Hast thou considered my servant Job,
a simple and upright man,
fearing God and avoiding evil
and still keeping his innocence
in spite of his afflictions?"
And Satan said:
"Skin for skin and all that a man hath
he will give for his life".
"But put forth thy hand
and touch his bone and his flesh
and then thou shalt see that he will
bless thee to thy face".
And the Lord said to Satan:
"Behold, he is in thy hand;
but yet spare his life".

(iv)

So Satan went forth
and struck Job with a grievous ulcer
from the sole of his foot

even to the top of his head.
And Job took a potsherd
and scraped the corrupt matter,
sitting on a dunghill.

(v)

And Job said:
"One thing there is that I have spoken,
both the innocent and the wicked
doth the Lord consume"
"I will speak and I will not fear him
for I cannot answer while I am in fear"
"I will say to God:
'Tell me why thou judgest me so'.
'Doth it seem good to thee
that thou shouldst calumniate me
and oppress me, the work of thy own hands
and help the counsel of the wicked?'"

(vi)

Then the Lord answered Job
out of a whirlwind and said:

"Who is this that wrappeth up
sentences in unskilful words?"
"Where wast thou
when I laid the foundations of the earth?"

(vii)

Then Job answered the Lord
and said:
"I know that thou canst do all things
and no thought is hid from thee".
"With the hearing of the ear
I have heard thee but now
my eye seeth thee"
"Therefore I reprehend myself
and do penance in dust and ashes".

(viii)

And the Lord accepted the face of Job
and much as they had begun
so did Job's torments end.
And the Lord gave Job twice as much
as before, blessing his latter end
more than his beginning.

And Job lived after these things
a hundred and forty years
and he saw his children
and his children's children
unto the fourth generation.
And he died, an old man
and full of days.

(ix)

And yet ...

A Long Talk With Lucifer

Knows everything,
as you wr ld expect.
Remembers each detail
of that interminable, blazing fall.
Is beginning to forget,
with a deep and terrifying regret,
the face of God.

Too Lovely For Words

Strange to say
I was elbow deep in the dictionary
when you called.
Looking up the precise meaning
of "exquisite".
"Your exquisite face etcetera, etcetera..."
"Stunned into heart-troubled silence
by your exquisite, whatever..."
And then, of course,
your brush-fire hair
your eyes of needles and candles
your ears of tremors and rumours
your nose of lemon and cardamom
your mouth of honey and infamy
your tongue of nightmare and ravings
your voice of sudden tumultuous
announcements in the wilderness
your neck of birch and whispers
your throat of shuddering guitars
your shoulders of feathers and tendons
your back of ebony and lamentations

your arms of spanners and cables
your hands of paper and thunder
your fingers of salmon and destiny
your breasts of apples and planets
your belly of wheat and lightning
your buttocks of pure gold
your thighs of hammers and demons
your vulva of crevice and cleft of
fern shaded rock pools deep in the forest
of burning afternoons
your legs of seraph and antelope
your ankles of poise and desire
your feet of distance and dreaming
your exquisite toes.

The Big Issues

Word comes through
that you are working your ass off.
If there is one as lovely
in the teeming seraglio
of a Turkish soccer player,
I'll eat my fez.
If there are breasts
more shapely beneath the vests
of Mao's fearless militia women,
I'll swallow my little red book.

Niamh In Doheny & Nesbitt's

When you came into the bar
that Sunday afternoon,
the entire clientele
tilted precariously on their stools
to steal a glimpse
of your spellbinding beauty.
When you reached across the counter
to collect your pint and crisps,
creaking in those poured-into denims,
the famous stopped clock shuddered
and began to click again.

Welcome to oblivion.

Haiku With Cap And Bells

In an open grave
the gravedigger putrefies
none to cover him.

Bell's Field Haiku

(for Sarah Durcan)

A housefly sunbathes
on the glossy verandah
of an ivy leaf.

A sullen cloud mass
drags grey underskirts of rain
along the river.

A belfry starts up
a sweet iron clamouring
swells from the city.

Oh Fuck Off

No mention in the morning clarion
of the miraculous appearance of the image
of an image of the Blessed Virgin in raised pastry
on a chicken and mushroom pie in a fish and
chip shop on the South Douglas Road or of the vast
and already heaving multitudes quickly bussed into
place and intoning decade after decade of the rosary
or of the swivelling dick-head dead Elvis lookalike
who purchased the marvellous pie and insisted
upon his right to consume it there and then
much to the chagrin of the murmuring throng.

And yes you do get tired of it all the entire
or at least the observable universe and the
aloof orbital indifference of the planets and the
grotesque distances between stars and the eternal
oscillation between expansion and contraction
and the growing realization that everything you
have said and done up to now with the
understandable exception of an evening alone
in the paradisal shadows of the Alhambra may
be part of an extremely elaborate dream you

are having in your tipsy mother's womb or
the awful possibility that you are already a
thousand years dead and haunting the shattered
empty shell of your self and the grim
probability that it would have been infinitely
better for all concerned if you had never been
born in fact it would solve everything for
once and for all if someone could arrange
to send that little Dutch fucker back through
a wormhole in the space-time continuum
to stick his finger in the Big Bang.

This is the fourth time I have met that
end of the world is nigher idiot the day after
his predicted end of the world whimper and this
is the fourth time he has justified the non-event with
the pompous declaration that to all intents and
purposes the world ended ages ago with
the awareness of the interminable recycling
of history and the whirling momentum of
time and just as I am beginning to think
that he is right after all I read in the evening
bugle that this very same prick in the furze
has won the lotto I mean even to do the lotto.

Portents Portents

A good omen,
the robin coming into view,
is trying to overtake
a bad omen,
the crow disappearing from sight.
My mother croaks
clutching her lottery ticket.

One Melville Terrace
(for Hugh)

Who knows?
A hundred years from now
I may still be here.
A swallow flitting in and out
through warping roof-beams,
or a rat scrambling across
a jumble of worm-eaten books,
unremittingly cheerful.

Dispersal

When I am finally
burned to a crisp,
pounded to a fine ash by steam-hammers
and scattered from south-facing cliffs
over a disconsolate sea,
I would hope
that at least one fundamental particle
of my being could occasionally recycle
to the sunlit shallows below Myrtleville,
there to swirl playfully
around your thousand year old feet.

Haiku for Norman MacCaig

The bittern's lament
recalling the giddy soul
to its loneliness

Boabdil's Moon

The moon's first quarter
has risen over the Alhambra.
It is poised like a scimitar
above the city of Granada.

Paseo

(I.M. Federico Garcia Lorca)

I almost envy you
that pre-dawn stroll beyond Víznar.
The firing squad, eagerly preparing
to rid Holy Spain of four more reds,
is taking careful aim at your backs.
An early breeze is making mischief
amongst the pines.
I can imagine
that half-terrified, half-fascinated
look over your shoulder
as you wonder
if the old adage holds true:
that you will not hear the bullet
that kills you.
The headlights of the trucks
keep you targeted
until the fusillade crashes out,
calling a halt to your final paseo.

You Did. And You Did.

A blank page in eternity to you Berryman
and Dante (and Virgil)
to greet you on the other side.
An honoured place in the First Circle
and the fee waved graciously aside
by the ferryman.

The Complete Works Of Samuel Beckett

is is?
was is?

was was?